From Snark to Bark

Sassy Thoughts From Your Pup

M. S. Gregory

Copyright © 2025
by Tried and Trusted Indie Publishing

ISBN:
All rights reserved.
Cover designed by msgdragon

No part of this publication may be reproduced, distributed, or transmitted in any form or by any means, including photocopying, recording, or other electronic or mechanical methods, without the prior written permission of the author, except non-commercial uses permitted by copyright law

Also by M. Gregory

Cousin Chaos: Laughing with your Cousins
- Sibling Shenanigans: Laughing with my Sister
- Sibling Shenanigans: Brother-Sister Jokes
- Mum Seriously!! Teen-mum banter at its finest!
- What Cats really Think: Hilarious Cat Thoughts, Jokes, and Conversations That Will Make You Laugh

For permission requests, address the request to the author c/o
Permissions,
TAT Indie Publishing
triedandtrustedindie@gmail.com

"My human says I need obedience training... I say they need snack distribution training."

"Every time they open a bag of chips, I suddenly remember how to sit, stay, and roll over."

"They call it a walk. I call it a chance to pee on everything I own."

"My human thinks they're feeding me. I think they're performing a daily magic trick... disappearing food into my belly."

"They say, 'No begging at the table.' I say, 'Challenge accepted.'"

"I don't fetch sticks. I fetch their self-esteem… they drop it every time I ignore them."

"Bath time is when my human learns that I can run faster than their reflexes."

"They say 'good boy!' like it's a compliment. I know I'm just making them feel important."

"I wag my tail when they come home. Mostly to distract them while I steal their socks."

"My human claims they walk me. Truth: I walk them… straight into puddles and mud."

"I bark at the mailman, the cat next door, and sometimes the vacuum... just to remind my human I'm doing my job."

"They bought a fancy dog bed. I sleep on the floor, just to assert dominance."

"My human calls me their best friend. I call them my treat dispenser."

"They teach me tricks. I teach them patience... mostly through shedding."

"Every time they put on shoes, I pretend I don't care... then follow them like a shadow."

"My human bought a ball. I pretend to chase it... just to see them throw it again."

"They try to cuddle with me. I allow it... on my terms, of course."

"My human laughs when I roll in mud. I laugh too... at their ruined laundry."

"I bark at 3 AM. My human calls it annoying. I call it ensuring they're awake for breakfast."

"They think I'm affectionate. I'm just strategically placing my head on their lap... for treats."

"Oh, you wanted me to sit? Cute. I was just pretending to listen while plotting your embarrassment at the vet."

"You call it a leash. I call it your attempt at controlling pure chaos... good luck."

"You bought me a squeaky toy. I squeak it once, then judge your life choices quietly."

"You dress up for work, but I'm the one making the living room carpet my runway."

"You think you trained me to stay off the couch? That couch chose me."

"You yell 'no!' like it matters. I've already ignored smarter humans than you."

"You say 'who's a good boy?' I say: who's the one leaving crumbs on the floor?"

"You take me for walks like it's exercise. I call it an opportunity to judge your sense of direction."

"You bought a dog bed. I sleep on your side anyway. Sorry, not sorry."

"You call it obedience. I call it tolerating your weird rituals— like yoga... naked humans stretching is scary, by the way."

"You say you rescued me. I say I'm training you to open cans like a pro."

"You try to make me behave at the park. Meanwhile, I'm socially ranking every human here."

"You think the mailman is a threat? Cute. You've met me—true chaos lives here."

"You say 'stay' but look at you—can't even stay awake past 10 PM without snacks."

"You're worried about me chewing shoes? Please. Your taste in footwear is worse than my chewing."

"You give me a bath. I give you a makeover… mud, leaves, and lots of hair."

"You talk about your diet. I talk about mine: leftover pizza crusts and your stunned reaction."

"You hide when I bark. Please. I bark because you're boring."

"You think I'm attached to you. Sweetheart, I'm attached to the treat bag—and maybe your Wi-Fi."

"You think you're walking me? Cute. I choose the route, you just follow and look busy."

"You call it 'feeding time.' I call it 'human fumbling with the food container again.'"

"You bought a squeaky toy. I hide it immediately to watch your stress rise."

"You say 'heel!' I say, 'I'm in charge of pacing, thank you very much.'"

"You left the house for five minutes. I've already planned a full-scale furniture investigation."

"You think I don't understand you. I understand perfectly. I just don't care."

"You try to ignore me while I stare. Cute. I'm training your guilt muscles."

"You dress up for Zoom calls. I dress up your carpet in fur and mud."

"You say 'drop it!' I say, 'Never. Consider it a negotiation lesson.'"

"You bought a new rug. I consider it my canvas for artistic shedding."

"You say 'quiet!' I say, 'I bark because the world is boring, and so are you.'"

"You try to hide from me in the shower. Adorable. I've already figured out the acoustics."

"You say 'stay.' I stay... until I feel like asserting dominance again."

"You talk about going for a run. I talk about the nap I'll take while you're gone."

"You bought a doggy sweater. I wear it once and then nap in defiance."

"You say 'come!' I pretend to think about it... then saunter slowly, judging your timing."

"You're proud of your new shoes. I'm proud of the holes I'm about to make in them."

"You say 'no jumping!' I say, 'Did you forget I own the furniture?'"

"You yell at me for shedding. I call it a seasonal contribution to your interior décor."

"You try to brush me. I treat it like an interrogation... and then shed on your lap in protest."

"You say 'bedtime.' I say, 'We'll negotiate... I take the bed, you take the floor.'"

"You call me your best friend. I call you my unpaid personal chef and chauffeur."

"You bought me treats. I act grateful, but really, I'm testing your generosity."

"You say 'no begging!' I say, 'Challenge accepted—and I've got a strategy.'"

"You try to hide the remote. Cute. I've been watching your panic for years."

"You call it obedience training. I call it an opportunity to mess with your pride."

"You say 'don't chew that!' I say, 'Your shoes begged for it.'"

"You think I'm excited to see you? Nope, I'm just calculating where the snacks are."

"You bought a leash. I call it a suggestion box."

"You try to ignore me while I stare. Joke's on you—I'm in your head now."

"You say 'good dog!' I say, 'You're only impressed because I let you be.'"

"You bought a pet bed. I treat it like a recommendation for where you should sit."

"You call it a walk. I call it a sniff-and-judge-the-neighbors tour."

"You put me in the car. I act thrilled. I'm actually judging your driving skills."

"You yell 'stop!' I act surprised... while secretly planning my next chaos move."

"You bought me a toy. I hide it. Then I watch your stress levels rise like a spectator sport."

"You say 'stay!' I stay... long enough to test how much patience you really have."

"You try to train me. I train you—in the fine art of bribery and guilt."

"You think I listen. I hear, but I selectively obey... based on snack availability."

"You clap when I do a trick. I clap back with extra fur on your couch."

"You say 'come here!' I take my sweet time... because I know you'll beg."

"You yell 'bath time!' I treat it like a full-scale protest."

"You talk about your day. I nod politely… while mentally planning the sock heist."

"You try to sneak food under the table. Amateur hour. I've got radar."

"You buy me fancy food. I prefer to judge the leftovers on your plate."

"You call me your protector. I call you my snack provider… mostly accurate."

"You say 'no furniture!' I say, 'I didn't hear you. Must've been the treats.'"

"You try to cuddle. I choose when it's convenient... mostly at 3 AM."

"You think I'm barking at nothing. Nope, just mentally noting your mistakes."

"You bought me a winter coat. I treat it like a fashion statement you have to admire."

"You say 'heel!' I say, 'I've got my own agenda, thank you very much.'"

"You call it a dog park. I call it a social commentary on your inadequate leadership."

"You say 'good boy' like I care. I care about the snacks."

"You think I follow commands. I follow snacks."

"You clean up my mess. I consider it performance art."

"You buy toys. I prefer boxes."

"You think you're in charge. Cute. I supervise you."

"You try to train me. I train your patience instead."

"You buy a new bed. I still claim the laundry basket."

"You yell when I dig. I dig because you lack excitement."

"You take me to the vet. I take revenge later on your slippers."

"You bought a treat jar. I test its security daily."

"You say 'quiet.' I say, 'Define quiet... human edition.'"

"You dress up for company. I dress up your couch in chaos."

"You say 'stay.' I stay... but my mind is free."

"You call it obedience. I call it selective compliance."